Landscape Touch
Vol. 3

Sun Mi Kwon

ABOUT THIS BOOK

Welcome to a visual journey designed to inspire outdoor living possibilities. This book is crafted with the vision of empowering new homeowners to curate outdoor spaces that resonate with their lifestyle, while offering contractors and architects fresh perspectives and innovative ideas to elevate their craft, portfolios, and businesses. It serves as a valuable educational resource for students striving for excellence in their projects. With stunning and distinctive night views illuminated by captivating lighting designs, this book stands out as a unique treasure in its genre. Join us now as we explore the realm of endless possibilities. May this book guide you towards achieving your desired outdoor oasis. Whether you choose to implement the entire design or incorporate select elements, you'll find endless inspiration to enhance your outdoor living experience.

TABLE OF CONTENTS

Day View

2D FLOOR PLAN VIEW

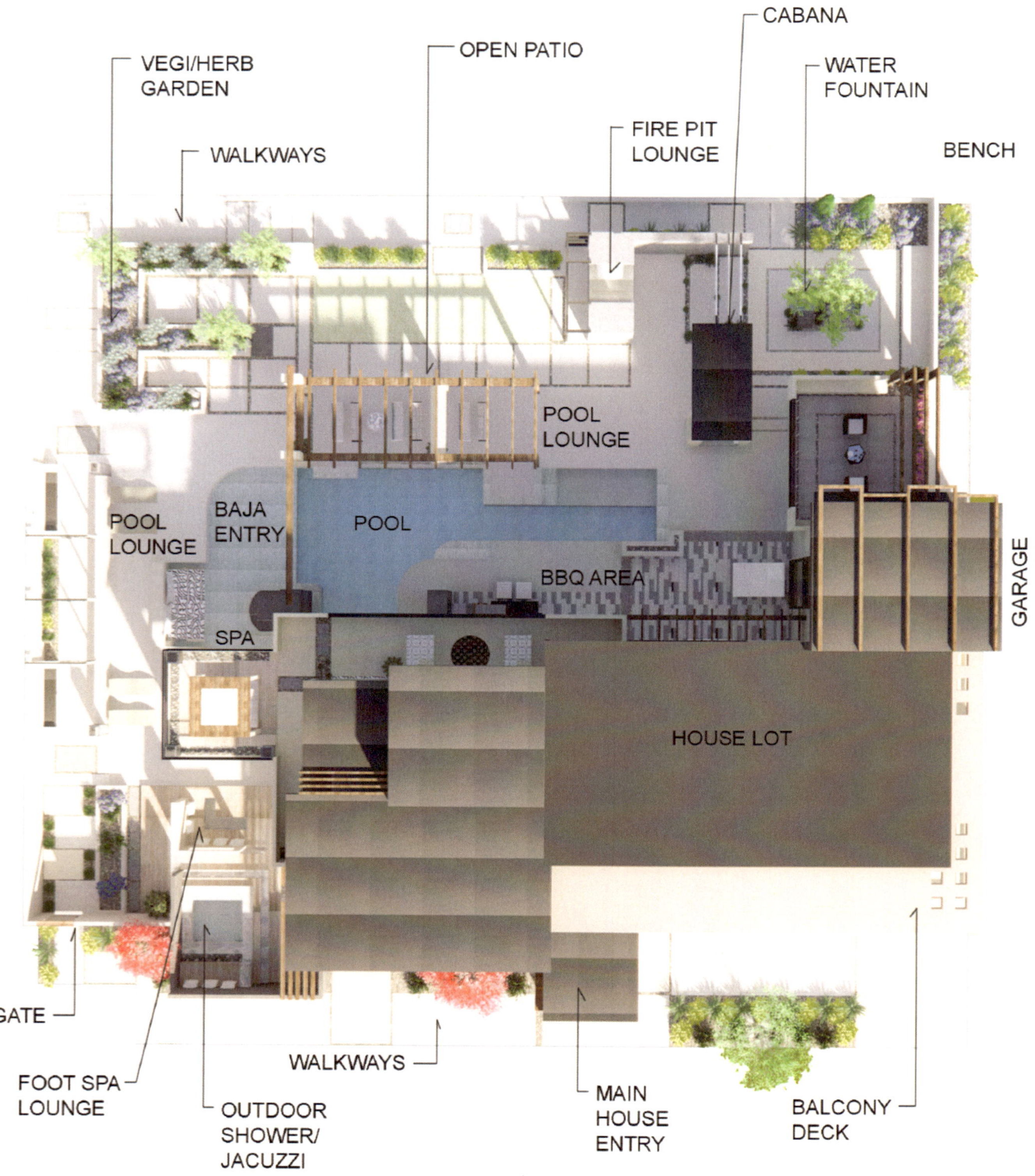

3D HOUSE VIEW 1

2ND FLOOR BALCONY W/FIRE PIT
GROUND LEVEL CALIFORNIA ROOM W/OUTDOOR KITCHEN & DINING LOUNGE AREA
2ND FLOOR OPEN DECK LOUNGE
BAJA LOUNGE
GROUND LEVEL CAR GARAGE W/OPTIONAL SHOW WINDOW
SWING BED CABANA
COURTYARD W/ ACCENT PLANTER

2ND FLOOR OPEN DECK
W/SWING BED CABANA
2ND FLOOR
CALIFORNIA ROOM
BACKYARD
ACCESS GATE
POOL DECK LOUNGE
W/HAMMOCK
BAJA W/ISLAND
LOUNGE, POOL &
SPA ACCESS
GARDEN
LOUNGE
W/HERB
GARDEN

HOUSE FRONT ISO VIEW

HOUSE RIGHT ISO VIEW

HOUSE LEFT ISO VIEW

MAIN HOUSE ENTRY
&
WALKWAY

HOUSE RIGHT SIDE WALKWAY TO GARAGE &
SIDE GATE ACCESS TO SIDE & BACKYARD

OPTIONAL ACCENT FIRE COLUMN

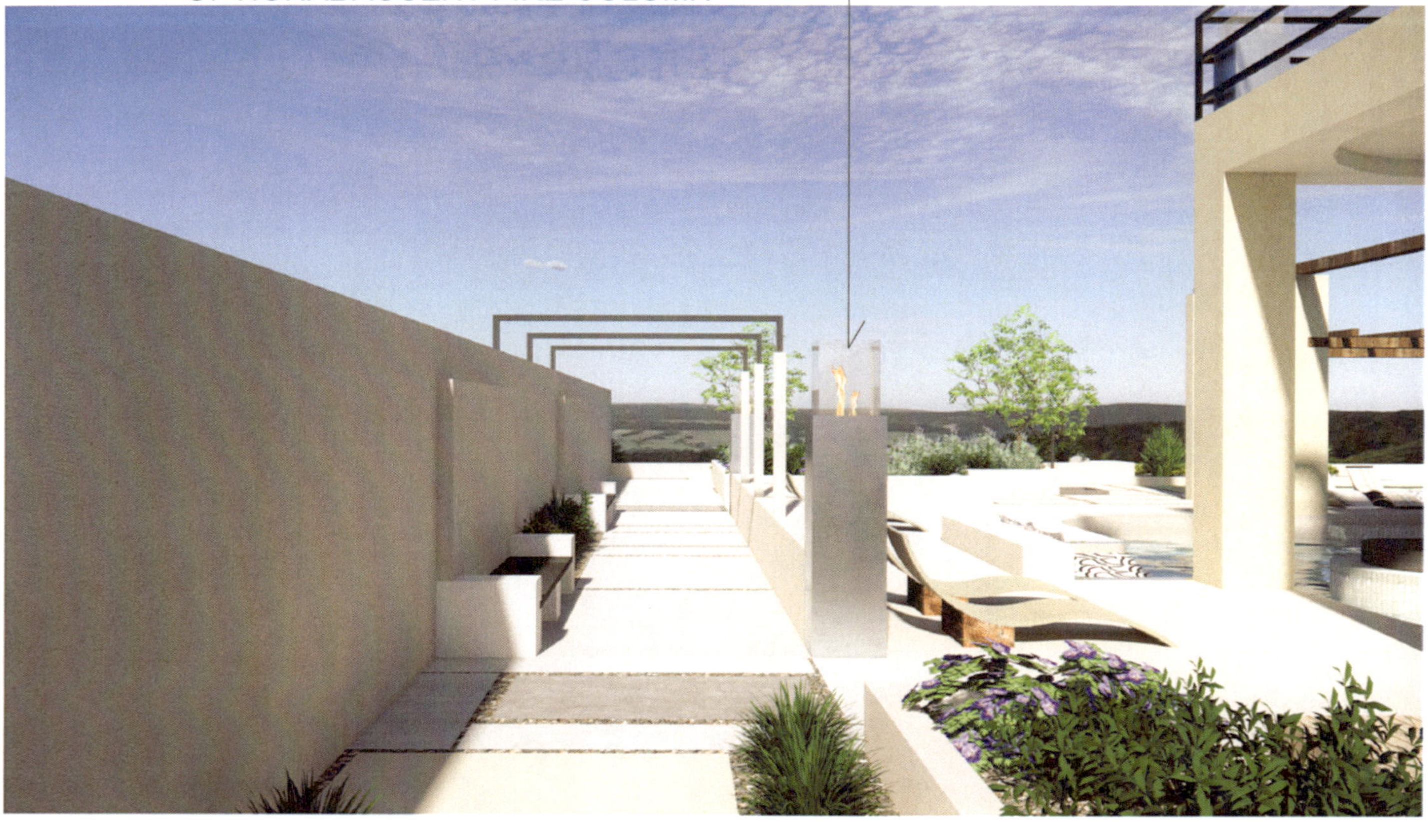

SIDE YARD ACCESS W/OVERHANG TRELLIS & SEATING BENCH

ACCENT STEEL FRAME
OVERHANG TRELLIS

WALKWAY VIEW FROM INSIDE OF THE GATE

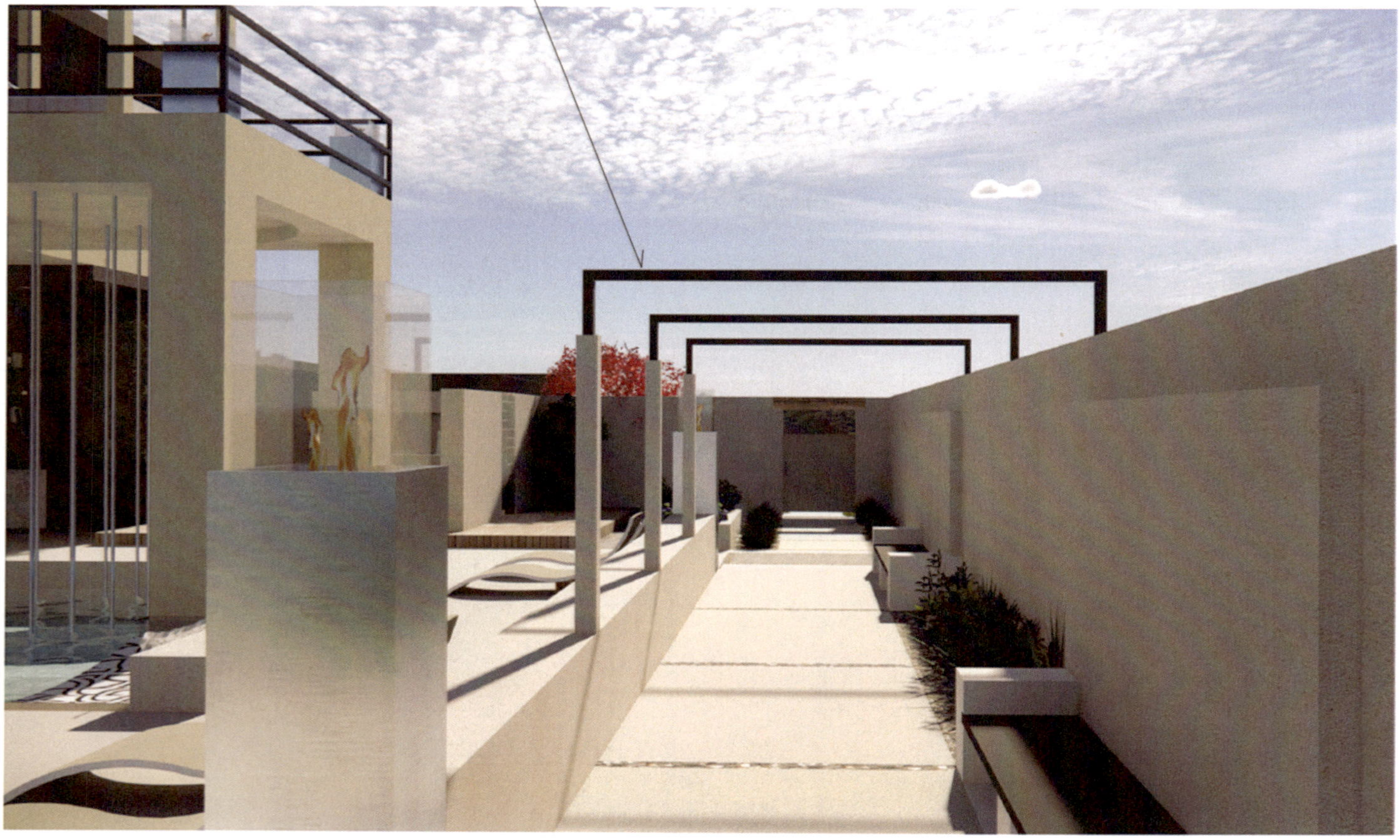

SIDE GATE & WALKWAY

W/PLANTER & PLANTER BOX

WASHED FINISH CONCRETE WALKWAY
W/LOOSE OR EMBEDDED PEBBLE BAND

FOOT SPA DECK W/ COMPOSITE DECKING

SMOOTH STUCCO AT SPA LOUNGE PARTITION/BACKING WALL

FOOT SPA LOUNGE W/ WOOD PLANK LOOK COMPOSITE DECKING

NATURAL STONE COPING & STEPS

JACUZZI & SHOWER OVER VIEW

PORCELAIN TILE VENEER AT SHOWER & SPA LOUNGE WALLS

JACUZZI & SHOWER OVER VIEW

CALIFORNIA ROOM MONUMENT STRUCTURAL WALL (BAR SIDE)

CALIFORNIA ROOM BAR & LOUNGE

POOL & WATER FEATURE AT SPA

POOL & SUBMERGE SPA AT BAJA LOUNGE

POOL & SPA W/POOL ISLAND LOUNGE

POOL BAJA & BAR LOUNGE AREA

POOL BAJA & BAR LOUNGE AREA

HAMMOCK LOUNGE@POOL BAJA LOUNGE

POOL COPING DECK LOUNGE W/FIRE PIT & PATIO COVER

SOLID CONCRETE COLUMN
W/OVERSIZED WOOD PATIO COVER

POOL ISLAND LOUNGE

HAMMOCK & ISLAND LOUNGE

POOL COPING DECK LOUNGE W/OPEN WOOD PATIO COVER & FIRE PIT

CALIFORNIA ROOM OUTDOOR KITCHEN, DINING & ENTERTAIN AREA NEXT TO POOL ACCESS

OUTDOOR KITCHEN W/DINING COUNTER & SMART TV

OUTDOOR KITCHEN W/DINING COUNTER & SMART TV

CALIFORNIA ROOM OUTDOOR KITCHEN
& DINING COUNTER

SWING BED POOL CABANA LOUNGE W/FIRE PIT

SWING BED POOL CABANA & ACCESS WALKWAY TO GARAGE VIEW

ACCENT WATER FOUNTAIN W/PLANTER & CABANA VIEW

OPTIONAL SHOW WINDOW GARAGE W/TEMPER GLASS 1"

CABANA SWING BED & WATER FOUNTAIN VIEW

WATER FOUNTAIN VIEW AT OPEN PATIO CABANA W/FIRE PIT

SWING BED & OPEN LOUNGE

LOUNGE COURTYARD FOUNTAIN

OPEN TRELLIS LOUNGE W/FIRE PIT

SWING BED CABANA
LOUNGE

OPEN LOUNGE
W/FIRE PIT

LOUNGE COURTYARD W/PLANTER

OVER VIEW / COURTYARD & LOUNGES

UPPER DECK VIEW

2ND FLOOR
OPEN DECK LOUNGE
W/ACCENT TRELLIS

2ND FLOOR
BALCONY LOUNGE

2ND FLOOR OPEN DECK LOUNGE
W/ACCENT TRELLIS COVER

2ND FLOOR BALCONY LOUNGE
W/FIRE PIT

2ND FLOOR BALCONY
SEATING AT RAIL

2ND FLOOR CALIFORNIA ROOM & OPEN DECK W/ SWING BED CABANA

SWING BED CABANA & LOUNGE

OVER VIEW UPPER & DOWN STAIR

POOL SIDE OPEN PATIO LOUNGE
W/FIRE PIT

GARDEN LOUNGE
W/HERB GARDEN

Night View

2D FLOOR PLAN VIEW

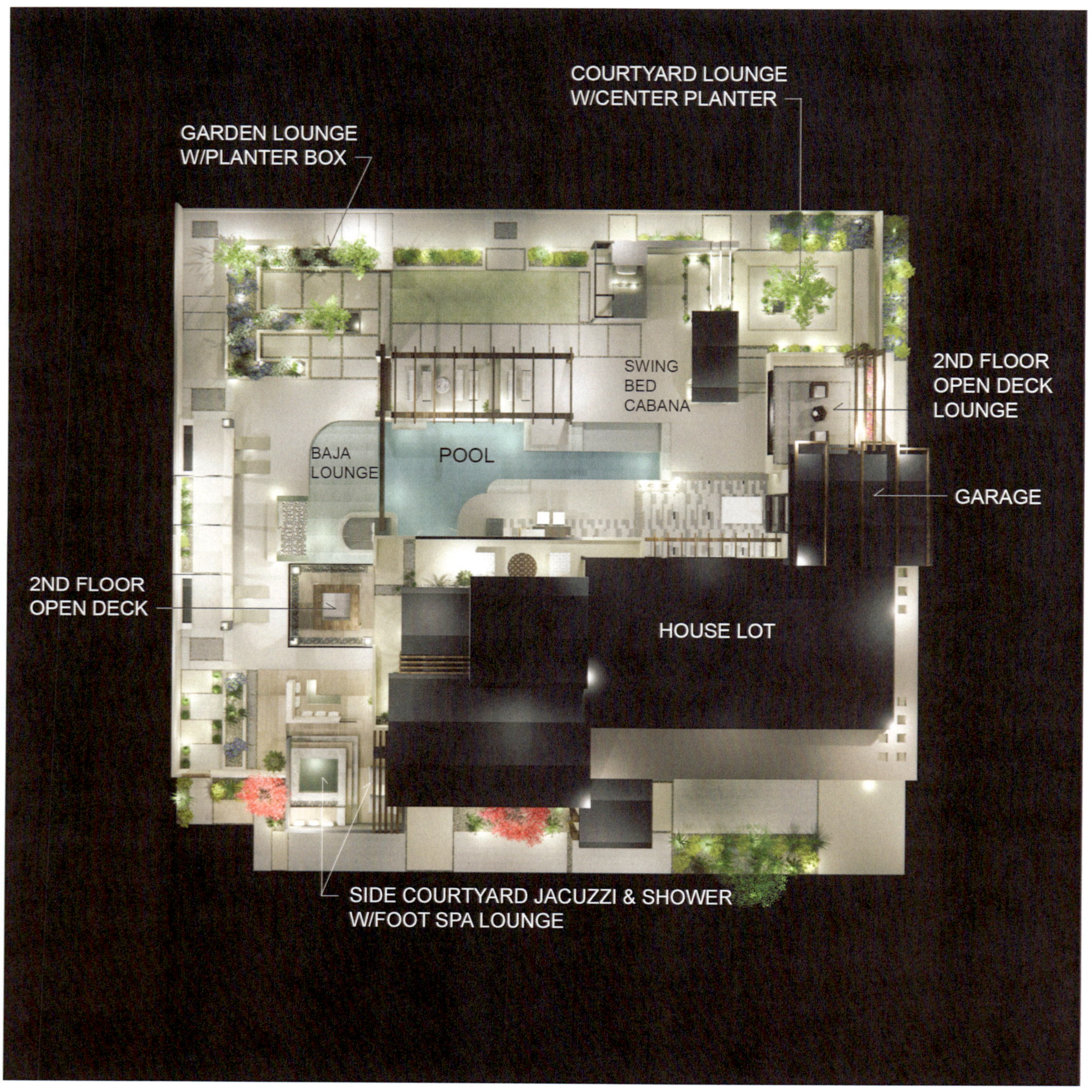

3D HOUSE NIGHT VIEW 1

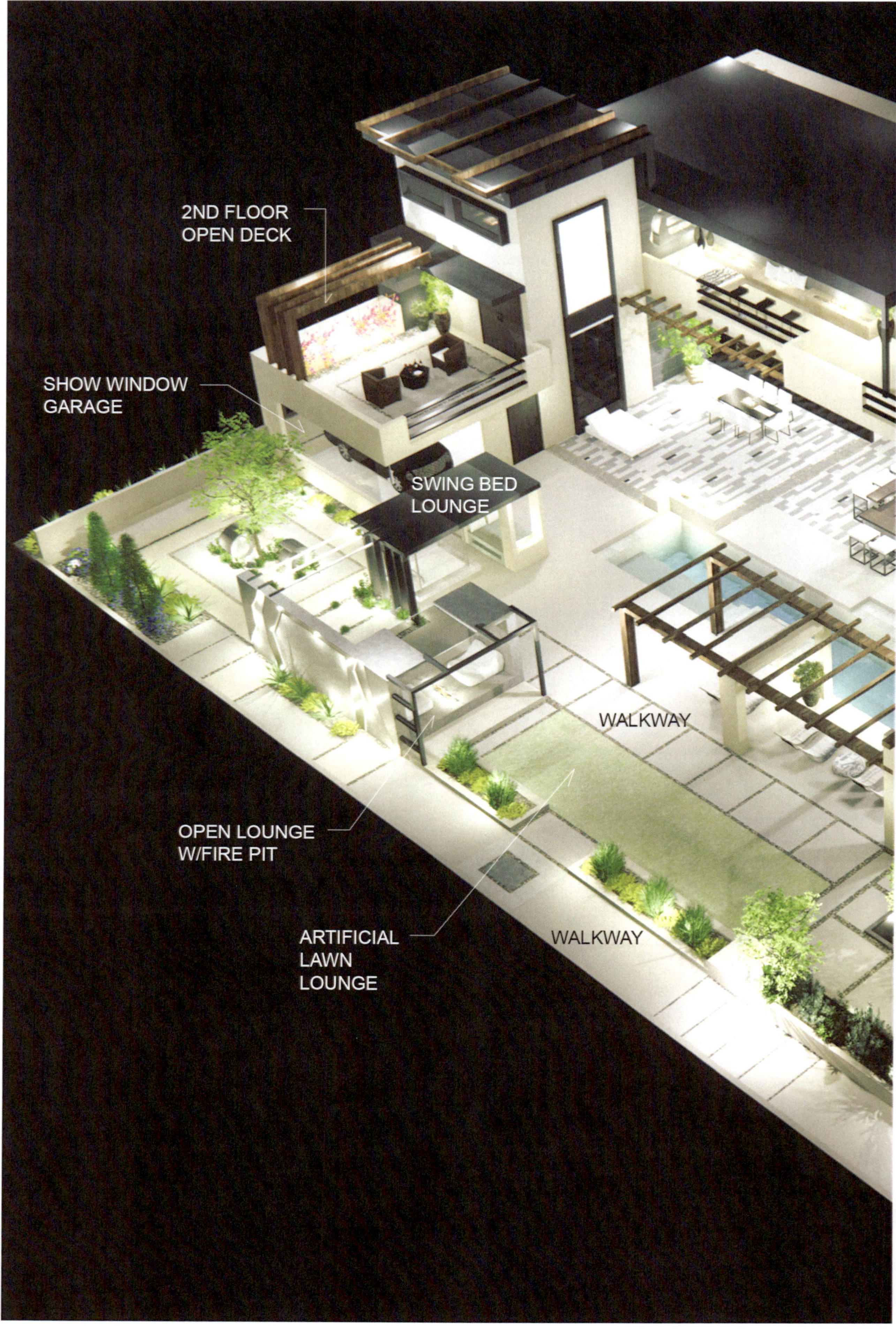
2ND FLOOR
OPEN DECK
SHOW WINDOW
GARAGE
SWING BED
LOUNGE
WALKWAY
OPEN LOUNGE
W/FIRE PIT
ARTIFICIAL
LAWN
LOUNGE
WALKWAY

BAJA LOUNGE
WALKWAY

3D HOUSE NIGHT VIEW 3

2ND FLOOR CALIFORNIA ROOM LOUNGE THEATER
JACUZZI/SHOWER LOUNGE AT GROUND LEVEL
SIDE & BACKYARD ACCESS GATE
ACCENT METAL FRAME TRELLIS
SPA W/ WATER FEATURE
GARDEN LOUNGE W/HERB GARDEN
POOL
BAJA LOUNGE
COPING DECK LOUNGE W/OPEN PATIO COVER
WALKWAY
WALKWAY
ARTIFICIAL LAWN & DAYBED LOUNGE
WALKWAY

HOUSE RIGHT ISO NIGHT VIEW

HOUSE FRONT ISO NIGHT VIEW

HOUSE FRONT LEFT ISO NIGHT VIEW

HOUSE SIDE WALKWAY & CAR GARAGE

MAIN HOUSE ENTRY VIEW

SIDE GATE & WALKWAY TO BACKYARD

SMOOTH STUCCO PARTITION WALL
W/CUT OUT

WOOD PLANK LOOK COMPOSIT DECKING
AT JACUZZI & FOOT SPA AREA

JACUZZI & SHOWER W/LOUNGE AREA

SUBMERGED SPA W/WATER FEATURE AT POOL BAJA LOUNGE AREA

POOL DECK & POOL ISLAND LOUNGE VIEW

POOL COPING LOUNGE W/FIRE PIT

NIGHT ENTERTAINMENT BAR & LOUNGE

POOL COPING LOUNGE W/HAMMOCK OVER THE POOL

OPEN PATIO POOL COPING LOUNGE W/FIRE PIT

POOL BAJA LOUNGE VIEW

POOL COPING LOUNGE VIEW

OPEN LOUNGE W/FIRE PIT & ACCENT TRELLIS COVER

FABRICATED METAL OR STONE ACCENT

SMOOTH STUCCO WALL W/OPTIONAL WALL ART DECO

OPEN LOUNGE W/FIRE PIT

COURTYARD W/WATER FOUNTAIN

SWING BED CABANA W/FIRE PIT

CALIFORNIA ROOM W/POOL ... 2ND FLOOR DECK & BALCONY LOUNGE VIEW

2ND FLOOR BALCONY LOUNGE W/FIRE PIT & SEATING

CALIFORNIA ROOM... OUTDOOR DINING & ENTERTAINMENT AREA VIEW

GROUND LEVEL CALIFORNIA ROOM KITCHEN & DINING

2ND FLOOR CALIFORNIA ROOM BALCONY LOUNGE

2ND FLOOR CALIFORNIA ROOM & OPEN DECK SWING BED CABANA

POOL ISLAND LOUNGE BY BAR ENTERTAINMENT AREA

SWING BED POOL CABANA VIEW W/OPTIONAL CAR GARAGE
SHOW WINDOW

ABOUT THE AUTHOR

Sun Mi Kwon brings over 23 years of experience as a living space and landscape designer, enriched by extensive hands-on expertise. With a robust background in on-site work, she possesses a deep understanding of practical landscape design principles. Throughout her career, Sun Mi has collaborated with a wide spectrum of clients, including private individuals, industry-independent contractors, and architects. Collectively, her contributions have led to the creation of over 1000 unique designs, showcasing her versatility and innovation in the field.